Midnight Lightning

Written by John Parsons

Illustrated by Rex Lightfoot

Contents	Page
Chapter 1. *Please don't tell Dad!*	4
Chapter 2. *The trolley is built*	10
Chapter 3. *Test drive*	15
Chapter 4. *Grampian Hills go-cart race 2000*	21
Chapter 5. *Next year awaits*	28
Verse	32

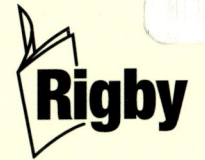

Midnight Lightning

With these characters...

Dad

Mom

Nicky

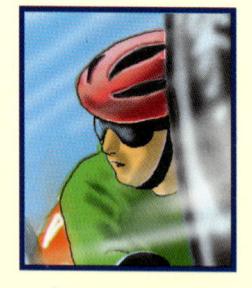

Helen Grizinski

"Grampian Hills Trolley

Setting the scene . . .

Nicky's dad is convinced that he is great at building and repairing things. But Nicky and his mother know better. Everything Dad touches is a disaster. So when a go-cart race is announced, Nicky is sure he is going to die of embarrassment in the go-cart he and his father will build. At first, everything seems to be going well—but a disastrous test run means that another plan is needed, and quickly!

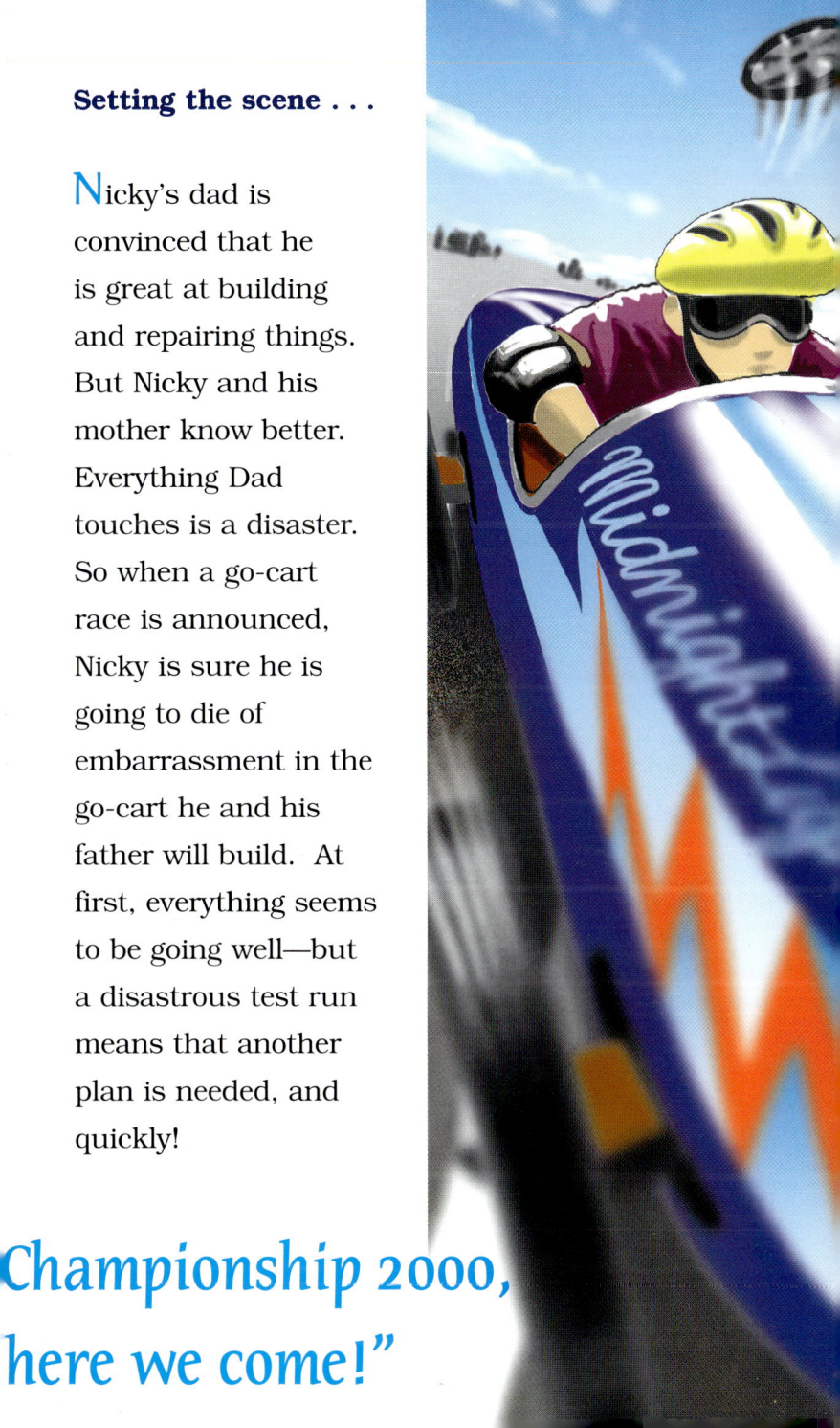

Championship 2000, here we come!"

Chapter 1.

"Don't tell Dad," I pleaded. "Please, *please* don't tell Dad!"

Mom looked at me sympathetically.

"You know he'll find out, Nicky," she warned.

I groaned. She was right, as usual. Dad would find out, and then there'd be no way out. I would be embarrassed, again.

"Well, can we keep it secret for as long as we can?" I asked hopefully. I really needed Mom's help!

Mom smiled and nodded. What a relief! If Dad discovered our secret, it would be a disaster—but this way, I might have a couple of days before the embarrassment started. Relaxing on the couch, I began to devise a plan.

I shouldn't have relaxed. By the time Dad returned home for lunch, he already knew. Helen Grizinski's father had told him. I was ruined!

"A go-cart race," he said breathlessly, dropping his bag of tools on the kitchen table.

Mom frowned at the toolbag as she had a hundred times before, but Dad was too excited to notice.

"There's going to be a go-cart race at the mall! Mr. Grizinski was putting up posters in his bakery this morning when I was buying breakfast there."

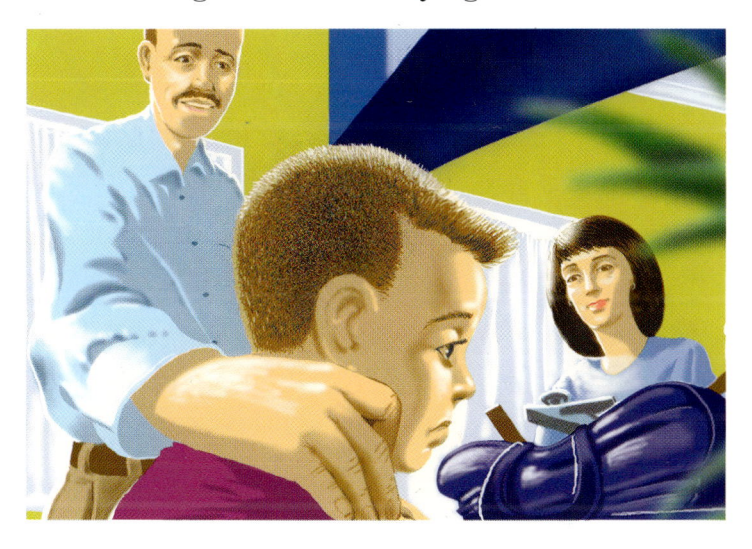

As my stomach turned, Dad came over and gave me a friendly thump on the shoulder.

"So, son, we need to get started if we're going to win! We need the best design, the strongest materials and the latest technology! We're going to design and build the *fastest* go-cart this suburb has ever seen!"

I buried my face in my hands. Mom gave me a sympathetic hug. Dad hopped from foot to foot. I felt a familiar gurgling feeling in my stomach. I was going to die of embarrassment!

As Dad chattered away excitedly, I considered the situation. Dad just loved to hide himself away in his workshop and build things. He was *enthusiastic*—there was never any doubt about that. But Dad was the most *hopeless* person I knew when it came to building anything.

Every weekend, when Dad tried to fix things around the house, the results were disastrous. Doors didn't close properly. Windows scraped and jammed. Tables and chairs wobbled more than before. Clouds of thick, black smoke belched out of the lawnmower after Dad had spent hours adjusting the engine. Even the car had refused to start after Dad had fiddled with the motor.

Mom would patiently try to repair everything Dad had worked on. She became an expert with screwdrivers, hammers and wrenches. Mom even went to evening classes to learn about carpentry, car repair, and plumbing so that she could fix Dad's 'repairs'. Dad just laughed at Mom.

"Why do you need to attend night classes to learn about those things?" he had wondered aloud. "You *can* consult your brilliant husband, you know."

Mom would give Dad a sarcastic look.

Today, she suggested a diplomatic solution to my problem.

"Maybe this time Nicky would like to build his own go-cart," she suggested.

"Nonsense," said Dad, beaming as he grabbed a microwave meal for lunch. "I guess you haven't heard about the Great Grampian Hills Go-Cart Race of 1972?"

Mom and I shook our heads in disbelief. We *hadn't* heard about it, but we knew we were about to.

"Old Midnight Lightning," whispered Dad proudly. "The best go-cart ever built!"

He placed his meal in the microwave, and pressed some buttons.

"It was the finest go-cart ever seen in our town," Dad continued.

Dad smiled as he remembered the go-cart he had built with his father almost thirty years before. "We worked solidly for weeks. All the other kids were awe-struck when we rolled it out on race day."

I was unimpressed. I could just imagine what happened next. If Dad had anything to do with building Midnight Lightning, it would have fallen apart before the race had even started.

"It was the fastest mean-machine on four wheels," boasted Dad, ignoring the glances that Mom and I were shooting at each other. "It had the latest design, the latest components. No one could even come close! It was sleek and speedy and shot down that hill like a bolt of lightning!"

The microwave beeped and Dad scraped his lunch from the plastic container onto his plate.

"And then what happened?" I asked, secretly thinking that it could *only* have been a disaster.

Dad sat up proudly, pulled in his stomach, and set his shoulders back.

"Well, your mother didn't know she married the Grampian Hills Go-Cart Champion of 1972," he said, glowing with pride.

Dad poked his fork into his meal. "This is still half-frozen," he murmured. "Remind me to take a look at the microwave on Saturday morning."

Mom made a mental note to enrol in a household appliance repair course as soon as possible.

Chapter 2.

There was nothing I could do now. Dad was determined to help me build a go-cart that would be the envy of every kid. Over the next week, he designed new plans for building the fastest go-cart in town. Dad raved about aerodynamics, velocity, and friction. He proudly showed off his sketches of ball bearings, steering systems, and springs.

On Saturday morning, after Dad had "repaired" our microwave, he bundled me into the car. Leaving a cloud of black smoke, we shuddered and bumped our way to the hardware store.

"I must check this engine again," said Dad as we pulled into a parking spot. "I think those guys at the service station have ruined it again."

"Sure, Dad," I said as I scanned the parking lot, hoping none of my friends had seen me in our pitiful car.

Dad raced around the hardware store, filling his shopping cart with nuts and bolts, metal, wire, wheels, pieces of wood and cans of paint. I followed behind glumly.

"These alloy wheels are lighter," Dad pointed out excitedly. "But these ones have a wider tread. We'll have to test both kinds under race conditions."

I nodded and asked if I could disappear outside and hang around the hamburger stand. But Dad wouldn't hear of it.

"There's work to do," he said seriously. "We have only two weeks until the go-cart race. Everything must be ready for a test drive next Saturday!"

He rushed into the next aisle. "Shall we get rope or nylon cord for the steering?" he asked, looking perplexed. I shrugged my shoulders. How should I know? Dad grabbed coils of both.

"Just in case," he said, winking. He was behaving like a big kid.

The next week I didn't see my friends at all—it was terrible. Every night, Dad dragged me into his workshop and we worked for what seemed like an eternity!

"Midnight Lightning Two," he said. "That's what we'll call her! It'll be the latest in a fine family tradition!"

It'll be the latest in a tradition of family flops, I thought grimly. But, as the week progressed, even *I* had to admit that Midnight Lightning Two looked promising.

Mom refused to enter Dad's workshop. She complained that it was a disgrace and looked like a trash heap. Dad would look up at her from the clutter of tools, the coils of wire, the pieces of bent metal and broken wood, and the buckets full of brightly colored electrical pieces.

"But I know where everything is," he would protest. "It's tidy, really."

On Friday evening, the day before our road test, Dad and I wheeled out our go-cart. Dad seemed about to burst with excitement.

He really was proud of our achievement. Even *I* thought we might have a chance of winning. Midnight Lightning Two *did* look impressive.

We had chosen the alloy wheels and used the most expensive grease Dad could buy at the gas station.

"The less friction, the faster it'll go," he pointed out. Mom nodded.

"With that pointy front, it'll cut through the air like a knife through butter," explained Dad. "Air resistance can slow a go-cart down by a mile per hour if you're not careful!"

"Really?" said Mom, pretending to be impressed.

"We have a double-steering system," he continued. "We have pedals for the rear two wheels, and we have a rope system for the front two wheels."

Mom smiled and tried not to yawn.

"That means extra control at high speed," Dad explained. "We'll need it. Midnight Lightning Two will be like a *supersonic* go-cart—the best ever seen in Grampian Hills!"

Dad looked confident as he stared at the magnificent machine we had created. Best of all, we painted it metallic blue—and on the front we painted a ferocious-looking row of shark's teeth.

"Psychology!" whispered Dad to Mom. "The opposition needs to be *scared* of our go-cart!"

"What do you think, Nicky?" Mom asked me. I couldn't help but smile. Dad's enthusiasm was infectious.

"I think it's the coolest go-cart," I said. Dad and I shook hands proudly.

"Grampian Hills Go-Cart Championship 2000, here we come!"

Chapter 3.

Saturday was our test drive day. We carefully loaded Midnight Lightning Two onto the trailer and covered it with an old tarp. We didn't want the opposition to see our secret design.

Dad and I left the house at 6:00 A.M. to reach the shopping center parking lot before anybody parked there. The car lurched and shuddered its way up to the shopping center. We didn't need the tarp. It would have been impossible to see the go-cart through the smoke!

We unloaded Midnight Lightning Two, and I put on my gloves, helmet, goggles, kneepads and elbowpads. There was no one else around. Feeling like I was about to step into a Formula One race car, I made my way over to our machine. Sitting in the seat, I grasped the rope. I tested the rear steering.

"Steering is okay," I said.

"Wheels okay," said Dad, as he pushed the go-cart backward and forward quickly.

"Brakes okay," I said, testing the handbrake.

Dad jiggled the go-cart up and down. "Spring suspension okay," he reported.

We both took a deep breath.

"Ready?" he asked. I pulled down my goggles and gave him the thumbs-up sign.

As he pushed me down the slope of the parking lot, Midnight Lightning Two began to glide downhill. As I gathered speed, the springs under the body of the go-cart absorbed all the bumps. The wheels hissed as the grease warmed up and the go-cart moved faster. The ropes and pedals felt firm, and the go-cart maneuverd effortlessly. It really was a lot of fun!

I raced past the first set of parking lots with the wind rushing past my face. I carefully steered around a drain, and Midnight Lightning accelerated even more. The noise from the wheels grew louder and louder as they sped around. The shark's teeth on the front of the trolley looked fearsome as I raced past a power pole. Just as Dad promised, the pointed front of the go-cart sliced through the air. I concentrated so intently on the asphalt ahead that I didn't feel the tiny vibration starting—until it was too late!

One of my rear wheels was coming loose!

The vibration turned into a shudder, followed by a crazy thumping sound. Midnight Lightning Two swerved all over the asphalt. Then, with a crash, a back corner of the go-cart hit the ground. A sickening grinding sound echoed around the empty parking lot. The left rear wheel snapped off and I watched helplessly as it sped past me. I tugged on the handbrake and tried to slow down, but the go-cart careened out of control, tipping me over.

I was grateful for my protective clothing as I tumbled over the hard ground. There was a terrible crash and, when I finally sat up, I stared down toward the end of the parking lot.

There, in a crumpled heap, was Midnight Lightning Two. Our go-cart was destroyed. One of the other wheels was spinning around, like a coin, a few miles away. The front was buckled and hanging loose from the frame. Our go-cart was wrecked beyond repair.

Dad sprinted toward me.

"Are you okay?" he said breathlessly. He was really worried.

"I'm fine," I replied. "Thanks to this helmet and these pads."

When I stood up, Dad put his arm around my shoulder. "That's a relief," he said. We both stared at the wreckage. "Let's go home," Dad said sadly.

When Mom saw us drive into the garage with the pile of wreckage in the trailer, she rushed out looking extremely anxious.

"I'm okay, Mom," I said, trying to sound cheerful. "I'm not hurt."

Mom was furious with Dad, but I explained that it wasn't his fault.

"We both did our best, Mom. But it just didn't hold up at such a fast speed."

We went inside and sat at the kitchen table. Mom had been trying to repair the microwave while we had been out, and had the repair manual open on the table. Dad didn't even notice. He had a glum expression on his face.

"Well, it's only a go-cart race," Mom said, trying to cheer us up. "There'll be another one next year."

Suddenly, Dad's expression changed to a determined one and he declared, "This family does not give up! We *will* enter that race."

"But, Dad," I said. "How can we possibly rebuild Midnight Lightning Two in time? It's totally ruined."

Dad stood up and beckoned for us to follow him. We headed for the workshop.

Mom and I stood at the door as Dad clambered over a mountain of spare parts, boxes and pieces of discarded projects in the darkest corner of the workshop. He reached an old, brown tarp covered in years of dust. He grabbed a corner and gave an almighty tug.

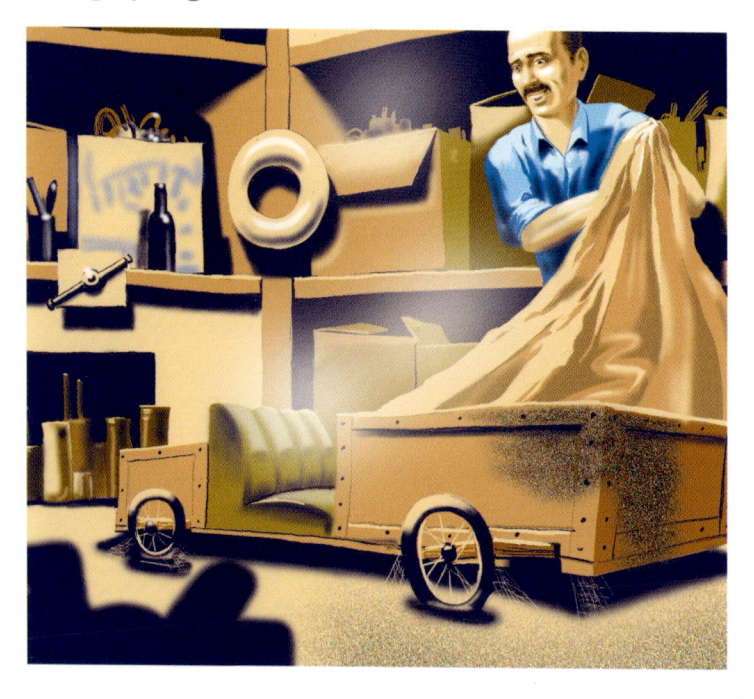

Mom and I stared in disbelief.

"We don't have to rebuild Midnight Lightning Two," said Dad enthusiastically. "We still have Midnight Lightning One!"

Chapter 4.

I stared at the dusty old go-cart that had been hidden for thirty years under the tarp. The way Dad had described it, I imagined that the original Midnight Lightning was almost as high-tech as Midnight Lightning Two. I blinked in disbelief at the old go-cart. It was nothing more than a battered, wooden apple box on a rusty iron frame. The wheels looked like ancient stroller wheels, with flat, gray tires. The spokes were covered with spider webs, and a strange blue-green fungus grew from the inside of the apple box.

"But ..." I sputtered, knowing that I couldn't *possibly* race in that antique.

"It doesn't look quite the way I remember it," admitted Dad. "But, with a little work, it'll be perfect. I just know it."

He cleared away the trash, and pushed the go-cart into the middle of the workshop. The wheels creaked and a spider crawled out from under the frame.

Dad brushed away the cobwebs, and I could see that the go-cart had once been painted a deep blue, just like Midnight Lightning Two. On one side, in faded red paint, was the name, Midnight Lightning. A shiver went up my spine. Was it a shiver of excitement or a shiver of dread? Surely Dad didn't expect me to race in that thing?

By the following Saturday, the weather was clear and sunny, perfect for a go-cart race. Dad and I had cleaned his old go-cart, greased the wheels, and repaired the rusty frame. There was enough paint left over from Midnight Lightning Two to repaint the old go-cart, and also to paint a set of shark's teeth on the apple box. I squeezed into the box, where my Dad had once proudly sat, and tested the new rope salvaged from our other go-cart wreck.

"Steering seems to work fine," I reported. When I pulled up the piece of wood that worked as a brake, it jammed against the rear left wheel. "Brakes will *probably* work," I said, not very confidently. Most likely, the go-cart would end up as wreckage at the end of the parking lot again, I thought glumly.

We loaded Midnight Lightning onto Dad's trailer and drove up to the shopping center. The parking lot had been cleared, and there were dozens of families already there. With a feeling of dread, I looked around at all the bright, glistening new go-carts.

Helen Grizinski had an awesome-looking machine painted red and yellow. She looked incredulous as we unloaded Midnight Lightning. "What's *that*?" she said, staring in disbelief.

I didn't answer. I wasn't going to let anybody see how embarrassed I was—mostly because I knew Dad would be upset.

At the starting line, the announcer shouted instructions into his megaphone.

"On the count of three," he explained, "each go-cart may receive a single push from their team members. Then, the first one across the line at the end of the parking lot is the winner. Be careful. Drive safely. Respect the other racers. And good luck to you all."

Sitting in my ancient apple box, I knew that last remark was aimed at me. I knew I would need all the luck I could muster just to make it down the hill safely. We hadn't had time to test drive Midnight Lightning!

"One ... two ... THREE!"

With an almighty shove from Dad, I was off. Immediately, all the other go-carts overtook me. Midnight Lightning creaked and rattled as it slowly rolled down the slope. Helen Grizinski's fabulous fluorescent machine sped into the lead. On either side, I could see the backs of the other go-carts as I was left behind. Every bone in my body was being shaken and jarred as I slowly rumbled down the car park slope.

But Midnight Lightning wasn't willing to give up just yet. After a few seconds, the wheels seemed to gather speed, and the steering rope tightened in my hands. Slowly, the old go-cart inched closer to the ones in front, and I held my breath as we rattled our way back into the pack. Midnight Lightning felt like she would shake herself apart, but she kept going, faster and faster.

Soon, there were fewer go-carts in front of me. I could imagine the surprise on the other drivers' faces as I clattered past them at high speed. But I didn't look left or right: I kept my eyes focused on that finish line, at the distant end of the parking lot.

The wheels squealed as we raced down the slope. Noise filled my ears and I gripped the steering rope tighter and tighter. The wind rushed past my face. Slowly but surely, the shark's teeth on Midnight Lightning edged closer to Helen Grizinski's fluorescent trolley. I saw her swiftly glance behind, and I grinned as I caught the look of disbelief on her face.

She leaned forward and urged her go-cart on.

I bent lower, too, and Midnight Lightning picked up even more speed. The go-carts on either side were a blur, and then they disappeared behind us. I was almost even with Helen Grizinski.

The finish line was getting closer and closer. I swerved to avoid a stone, and Helen Grizinski tried to veer in front of me. As I pulled in the opposite direction, Midnight Lightning obeyed my command like a Formula One race car. My whole body shook as we roared over the ground. Midnight Lightning seemed to come alive.

The shark's teeth inched their way in front of the fluorescent go-cart. We were locked in battle!

Helen Grizinski's cart moved back into the lead. I bent lower again and edged a couple of inches in front of her.

Then she snatched back the lead. In turn, I crept closer. We were neck and neck. Midnight Lightning surged forward again. From the corner of my eye, I could see a red fluorescent streak moving ever closer. Closing my eyes, I willed Midnight Lightning to make one last, supreme effort.

Chapter 5.

But as we raced past the finish line, I knew Helen Grizinski had pulled past us in the last few seconds. I pulled on the brake and coasted to a stop. I didn't care that we had come in second! What was truly amazing was that Midnight Lightning had held together after so many years. I looked back up the slope and spotted Dad and Mom running down toward me. From Dad's expression, you would have thought we had won. Mom's expression told me she was just glad I had survived! As I climbed out of the apple box, I was smothered in a huge double-hug!

"Magnificent!" said Dad breathlessly. "I would never have believed that old Midnight Lightning could match it with the best!"

"Congratulations!" said Mom excitedly. "You've both done a fabulous job!"

Even Helen Grizinski came up, shaking her head in disbelief.

"Wow!" she said. She looked at Midnight Lightning with admiration.

"It doesn't look like much but, boy, it can move. Who built it?" she asked.

"My dad," I said proudly, realizing that Dad was just about ready to burst again. He grinned broadly and put his hand on my shoulder.

"And you'd better watch out for us next year," he said confidently. "We'll be back."

The trip home in the car was noisy as everyone discussed every aspect of the race and every detail that could be improved next year. Dad was making a mental note of all the things we needed to buy from the hardware store to make Midnight Lightning faster than its modern competitors. I was thinking about driving tactics to make sure it reached the finish line even faster. Mom was driving and surprised Dad with her knowledge of building and technology ideas to speed up the old go-cart.

"I must have taught you well, dear," he said to Mom, while grinning at me. "It's lucky your mother is such a quick learner," he said. "Next year, we might even put her on the team."

Mom just laughed. She drove the car past the hardware store and pulled into the next set of stores.

"Why are we stopping here?" asked Dad. He looked back over his shoulder at the hardware store. "Shouldn't we be going in there?"

Mom shook her head and pointed at the appliance store in front of us.

"Not if you want any lunch today," she said, hopping out of the car. "You may be able to build the fastest go-cart in Grampian Hills, but you've completely wrecked our microwave."

"Microwaves!" laughed Dad. "They just don't build those things properly anymore." He turned to me. "Your mother didn't know she married the Grampian Hills Barbecue Cook of the Year, 1978," he said proudly. "*We* don't need microwaves."

Mom didn't have the heart to remind Dad that his barbecue had been in pieces since he had "repaired" it six months ago. I closed my eyes as they both went into the store to buy a new microwave. I was dreaming of the day when Midnight Lightning would once again roar towards that finish line ... FIRST!

"Awesome!"

Speed
Accelerating, exhilarating
Faster and faster
Wind through your hair
Awesome!